Growing Up
AMISH

∘◦●◦●◦∘

Books by Richard Ammon
THE KIDS' BOOK OF CHOCOLATE
GROWING UP AMISH

Growing Up
AMISH

°O°O°O°O°

RICHARD AMMON

Illustrated with photographs, maps, and drawings

ATHENEUM   1989   NEW YORK

PHOTO CREDITS

Dick Brown x, 62–63, 90–91, 94–95
Mel Horst title page, 3, 4, 10–11, 23, 28, 36, 37, 39, 69
Richard Ammon 7, 8, 24, 49, 71, 79, 86, 87

Atheneum
Macmillan Publishing Company
866 Third Avenue, New York, NY 10022
Collier Macmillan Canada, Inc.

First Edition
Printed in the United States of America
10 9 8 7 6 5 4 3 2 1

Library of Congress Cataloging-in-Publication Data
Ammon, Richard.
Growing up Amish/by Richard Ammon; illustrated with
photographs, maps, and drawings.—1st ed. p. cm.
Bibliography: p. Includes index.
Summary: Focuses on the homes, work, and schooling of a
Pennsylvania Dutch community to depict the Amish way of life.
ISBN 0–689–31387–X
1. Amish—Social life and customs—Juvenile literature
2. Pennsylvania Dutch—Social life and customs—Juvenile literature.
[1. Amish—Social life and customs. 2. Pennsylvania Dutch—Social
life and customs.] I. Title.
E184.M45A46 1989
973'.088287—dc19
88–27493 CIP AC

For Elizabeth and our Amish friends

CONTENTS

ACKNOWLEDGMENTS

I want to thank Dr. John Hostetler for his early-on encouragement and advice.

This book would have been impossible without my dear Amish friends, who helped simply by being themselves, practicing their beliefs.

I wish to thank Sara E. Fisher, a member of the Old Order Amish and a former schoolteacher and an author, who was kind enough to be the first reader of this book and give me several wonderful suggestions.

Thanks also go to Abner Beiler, also a member of the Old Order Amish, a consummate scholar and true friend, who gave the manuscript a most critical reading.

I especially want to thank Marcia Marshall for her timely support, insight, and encouragement.

ANNA'S DAY BEGINS

oᴏᴏᴏᴏᴏᴏᴏᴏ

A small light shines in the barn as Anna throws back the covers. Daat (Dad) has already stoked the wood stove downstairs in the kitchen so it isn't such a frosty surprise when she swings her feet onto the cold linoleum floor. *"Schteh uff,"* ("Get up") Anna says to her sister, snuggled under her heavy quilt, trying to deny morning.

Anna quickly slips into her brown work dress, for there are chores to be done before school. The animals are stirring. She hears the rooster greet the morning. A cow bellows.

Anna wears the same style clothing and does the same chores as her mother, grandmother, and great-grandmother before her. Change comes slowly to an Amish home and community.

Frieda, the family's wiry little terrier, escorts Anna to the barn. As Anna pushes back the barn door, she is greeted by two of the dozens of cats, all good mousers, that live in the barn. Inside, Daat calls, *"Gut Marriye,"* ("Good morning") over the growl of the diesel engine. Not so long ago the Amish milked their cows by hand. These days they milk with machines powered by diesel generators.

At a quick glance, you might not be able to tell an Amish farm from an "English" farm. But looking closely, you will notice no electrical or telephone wires strung from the lines along the road to the farmhouse and barn. And you won't see a TV antenna perched on the roof. Nor will you see any tractors in the fields. But you might see a windmill, which would be used to pump water.

It's not true that Amish will not accept any modern tools or appliances. They have no problems with pulling out a pocket calculator or using public telephones or the phone of one of their "English" neighbors. Why, Ben Stoltzfus even has a phone in his machine shop so he can call "English" businesses for parts. And if it happened that some Amishman used a pay phone to call Ben about fixing some machine and they talked a little about the weather or the crops, no one would say anything. But the phone must stay in the shop and not interfere with home life.

Amish use milking machines, and in the fields their horses pull hay balers powered by gas motors, but if you see a tractor in a shed, it's probably used for running a belt-driven machine such as a power saw. Some "liberal" Amish congregations permit the use of tractors in the fields, but only those with iron wheels.

Are the Amish just stubborn? Why do they make such a fuss over things that could make their jobs easier and quicker? Why do they look upon new gadgets with such great suspicion?

Before accepting or using a modern machine, Amish must be satisfied that this new thing will not interfere with their way of life. Although they have no objection to electricity, they are worried about all the things electricity can run, like radio and television. They would be worried about television programs that do not show examples of good Christian life.

When Anna, Levi, and Daat return to the house from milking, Mamm (Mom) has breakfast waiting. *"Gut Marriye,"* she says as they take their places at the big wooden table. Unlike many homes where family members eat breakfast alone or "on the run," grabbing a doughnut as they sail out the door, Amish families sit down together for a big breakfast.

Anna takes her place on the long bench. Beside her sit her younger sister, Rebecca, and her little sister, Sarah. Across the table, also on a long wooden bench, her little brother, David, sits next to Daat, followed by her older brothers, Levi and Amos.

Most Amish kitchens look just like this.

An Amish girl's bedroom. Notice the dresses hanging on pegs.

Anna's hungry. She has some fried cornmeal mush, a sunny-side up egg on top, some fried scrapple (pork and beef scraps mixed with cornmeal and seasoning), and a glass of milk. *"Geb acht,"* ("Be careful") Mamm warns, as Anna almost pours too much syrup on her mush.

Mamm, getting Anna more milk, Levi more scrapple, hardly has time to sit down herself. But she manages to take a few bites between all those turns to the stove and refrigerator.

Daat, sitting at one end of the table, talks mostly about what work needs to be done. Winter is a time for fixing things and getting organized for the long days of spring plowing. "The chicks might come today," he says.

Anna is excited. *"Sell iss gut!"* ("That is good!") she says.

"But first the brooder house must be made ready," Mamm says.

"You may do that, Anna," Levi says with a grin.

"Maybe I should do that right away," Mamm says. "Suppose the man from the hatchery should come this morning?"

Anna and Rebecca hurry upstairs to change for school. First, they make their beds, which stand side by side next to the window. There are no radios, stereos, or tape players, and no posters of rock stars decorate their bedroom. But above each bed the girls have tacked calendars with big pictures of horses.

Although some Amish hang their clothing on pegs, Anna and her sister hang only their bonnets on them. They hang their work dresses in the closet that was there when Daat bought the house from an "English" farmer. Before changing to her blue school dress, Anna gets a clean pair of stockings from the dresser that the two girls share. On top of their dresser, Anna and Rebecca display small hand-painted glass dishes they have received as gifts. One dish holds the white-headed pins that the girls use to fasten their capes and aprons to their dresses.

While Mamm fixes Rebecca's hair, Anna goes to the bathroom to brush her teeth. Then she combs her long hair. Amish women and girls do not cut their hair, ever. They do not even trim it.

Anna looks into the mirror above her dresser to make sure her part is right. Most older Old Order Amish cannot remember the time when they did not have mirrors. Girls and women use mirrors to fix their hair or make sure their prayer caps are on straight. Men use mirrors when shaving their upper lips. But they would never think of admiring themselves in a mirror.

After parting her hair, Anna pulls it back, twisting some strands along the side before fixing it into a bun. Over the years, all this tugging makes some women bald at the top of their forehead.

Anna puts on her black bonnet and coat, grabs her lunch box, and hustles down the long dirt lane with her brother Amos and her two sisters to wait for the school bus.

Clip-clop-clip-clop. A horse pulling a buggy prances over the ridge. As the team approaches, Anna waves. It's Uncle Abner! Maybe he's going to town or to the dry goods store up the valley. Anna wishes she could go with him to get some candy or pretty yarn.

Three crows fly from the naked oak as Abner passes. A cardinal pauses a moment on the fence post before flying over the stubble of the cornfield to look for forgotten kernels.

Living on a farm in the country, Anna is attuned to nature. Even on this frigid morning, she notices little signs of the coming of spring. Snow has melted in a ring around the maples lining the lane, telling her that the sap has started running. And this evening she will be able to complete her chores before sunset.

Anna hears a faint sound. She listens carefully, then points south in the sky. *"Guck, guck! Die Gens!"* ("Look, look! The geese!") she says to her brother and sisters. Spring is not far away.

Entering the valley is like traveling through a time tunnel. Farms and villages are cradled between two mountains that seem to shelter the people from much of the chaotic, fast-paced world of high tech, money, and politics.

A few years before Anna was born, her father could not find a farm in Lancaster County, where housing and industrial developments have covered much of the fertile farmland. So he and his brothers moved north, away from tourists, fast-food restaurants, and other fads and fashions that challenge their way of living.

One by one, Amish families began buying nearby farms, until today two church districts (congregations) fill the valley. When they moved here, many of these farms looked old, tired, and worn-out. But in a few years, and with a lot of hard work, the Amish fixed up their homes. First, they removed the telephone and electric wires, then painted the houses white, giving them a fresh, well-scrubbed look.

A stainless-steel tank truck crawls down the muddy lane to Uncle Levi's farm to collect milk for the dairy. Anna's brothers like to watch the shiny truck when it comes to their farm every other day.

The stainless-steel-tank milk truck comes to Amish farms every other day, but never on Sundays.

A Monday-morning clothesline waves with broadfalls and brightly colored dresses.

Then Anna hears the school bus straining up the hill as if it were complaining about carrying too many children. Soon it is in sight.

Anna takes a seat by the window. She can tell it's Monday morning by looking at the passing farmhouses. At each place hang clotheslines full of brightly colored dresses and shirts. Like headless scarecrows in a row, black broadfall pants seem to wave to her.

SCHOOL

oºOºOºOºOº

Children are playing outside the little white schoolhouse with its bell on top, running and shouting to one another. Anna jumps off the bus to tell her friends Rachel and Susie about the letter she received from her friend Elizabeth, an "Englisher."

Although Amish do business with "Englishers" practically every working day, they prefer no interference from outsiders and do not encourage or seek "English" friends. They take advice from 2 Corinthians 6:14.

> *Be ye not unequally yoked together with*
> *unbelievers: for what fellowship hath righteous-*
> *ness with unrighteousness? and what communion*
> *hath light with darkness?*

They see the rest of the world filled with wickedness. They call outsiders *anner Satt Leit* (the other sort of people), while referring to

9

Amish children arrive at school.

themselves as *unser Satt Leit* (our sort of people). Because Anna plays with Elizabeth whenever she comes to visit her grandmother, Elizabeth is valued as a trusted "Englisher" friend.

Soon the bell rings and thirty-six children, grades one through eight, quietly file into their one-room schoolhouse. Their teachers greets each child by name: "Good morning, Anna."

"Good morning, Fannie," says Anna. From oldest to youngest, from teacher to farmer to bishop, Amish call everyone by his or her first name. They do not believe anyone is better than anyone else just because of position or age.

Once inside, all the excited shouting turns to whispers. As they pass through the cool mudroom, the children place their lunch boxes on a shelf.

Bright pictures colored by the children decorate the walls of the classroom and mobiles hang from the ceiling, giving the modest room a warm, inviting atmosphere. The drawings of farms are not exactly alike, but they all look similar—a barn and a farmer plowing his fields. One boy, though, has drawn the farmer driving a bright red tractor!

Shoebox dioramas are stacked on a table near the sink. Each has a little square hole cut in the end. Inside each is a detailed farm scene, complete with miniature animals, people, and tractors.

A row of pegs lines the back of the room, each peg labeled with a child's name. The girls hang their bonnets and coats on the pegs and lay their folded black shawls on the shelf above. Girls younger than nine wear colored bonnets, often royal blue. Girls nine and up and women wear black bonnets.

The boys hang up their coats and black hats with wide brims. Boys younger than nine and men older than forty, as well as ministers, wear black hats with rounded crowns. Between nine and about forty, the boys and men wear black hats with a crease in the top.

Both boys and girls take off their rubber boots, clipping them together with a clothespin, and line up the pairs below their wraps.

While the children are hanging up their coats, Fannie stokes the fire. The first graders, who sit in the front, will soon be toasty warm. The seventh- and eighth-grade boys and girls, who sit in the last rows, farthest from the stove, might be a little chilly, but not uncomfortable. Anna sits in the middle with the other sixth graders.

Most of the children have done chores in the barn before coming to school, so there's a faint scent of horses mixed with the sweet aroma of body odor accenting the classroom.

At precisely eight-thirty Fannie taps the little bell on her desk and begins to take roll. In many public school classrooms it is not unusual for a few children to have the same first names. But in an Amish school it is not uncommon for some children to have the same first and last names. That's not hard to believe when you consider that there are only about a dozen first names for girls, a dozen for boys, and only a few more than a half-dozen family names—King, Kauffman, Fisher, Stoltzfus, Esh, Lapp, and Beiler. Fannie calls out, "Malinda, Rachel, Katie . . . Jake, Aaron, Amos. . . ." In school, children with the same names are often distinguished by their middle initial. Fannie calls two first graders, "Henry K. Esh" and "Henry B. Esh." By the time they

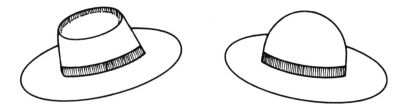

Boys younger than nine and men over forty as well as ministers wear black hats with curved, uncreased crowns. Between nine and forty, the men and boys wear black hats with creases along the edge that flatten the crowns.

grow up, they will probably acquire nicknames. In the valley, a father and son are called Young Ben and Old Ben, two Jakes are known for their physical characteristics—Strong Jake and Curly Jake—and Bishop Levi and Pepper Levi are named for things they do.

Like most Amish teachers, Fannie is young, in her early twenties. Unlike public school teachers, she did not go to college. In fact, she did not even attend high school. Like all Amish she completed only the eighth grade. Because she was a good student, she was asked to be an Amish teacher.

Children in Pennsylvania are expected to attend school until their seventeenth birthdays (or age sixteen, with parental permission and a full-time job). But in 1955 the state and the Amish compromised: Amish children are required to attend school only through the eighth grade. The following year and until they are fifteen, they go to school one half day a week to study advanced classes in German (so they can read their Bibles, printed in German), spelling, and arithmetic. They also keep a journal of their work. Mostly, like in an on-the-job training program, young future farmers help their fathers around the farm.

Partly because farmland is so expensive, some Amish have found other ways to make a living, becoming carpenters, harness makers, diesel mechanics, farriers, and dry goods storekeepers. So today young men have some choices. Levi wants to become a carpenter. Every day he goes off to work with an Amish carpenter, Samuel King. His diary tells what he learned about carpentry.

Girls have only two choices: A good student may become a schoolteacher. Most will become housekeepers. And as soon as a schoolteacher gets married and has a family, she, too, will stay home. Girls keep journals about home-making skills.

The question of allowing the Amish to maintain their own schools wasn't resolved until 1972 in the Supreme Court. In the case of *Wisconsin v. Yoder*, the high court ruled that states may not force the Amish to send their children to public schools. In an earlier, similar case in Iowa, Governor Hughes said, "I am more willing to bend laws and logic than human beings. I will always believe that Iowa and America are big enough in space and spirit to provide a kindly place for all good people, regardless of race or creed."

Amish do not believe in high school or college. All anyone needs, they feel, is to be able to read a newspaper and calculate the finances of the farm. They do not believe that education and knowledge make you a better person.

Fannie begins the school day by reading from the Bible. There is no discussion or interpretation of the verses. The Amish believe that Christianity should be lived, not talked about.

The students do not pledge allegiance to the flag. In fact, there is no flag in the classroom. The Amish do not believe in submitting to any government—the United States or Canadian governments or local governments. This belief stems from their mistreatment long ago by governments in Europe.

A few communities have special arrangements in which the Amish attend public schools just for them. Technically, "English" children are allowed to go to these schools, too, but none has chosen to do so. Because these are public schools, there are flags in the classrooms and the Amish children are required to say the pledge of allegiance.

∞∞∞

One way the Amish practice their faith is by following Christ's teaching in Matthew 5:39.

> *Do not resist one who is evil. But if any one strikes you on the right cheek, turn to him the other, also.*

While an Amish person may become angry, he or she will not fight. Usually, at the hint of a dispute between two people, an Amish person will become silent, ignoring the other person. Amish have been known to move away rather than face a fight, and it is rare for them to appear in court. As pacifists, people who believe in peaceful living, an Amishman would never think of going to war.

∞∞

JACOB AMMANN

‑oꞏOꞏOꞏOꞏOꞏo

Just as Lutherans are named after their founder, Martin Luther, the Amish take their name from their founder, Jacob Ammann. Little is known about Ammann. But by piecing together snippets of information, historians believe he was born in 1656 to a Swiss couple, Jacob and Katharina Ammann. A hard-working student, Ammann finished school a year ahead of those his age and was rewarded with a Bible. Later, probably when Ammann moved from Switzerland to Alsace, France, he became a member of the Swiss Brethren, religious followers of Menno Simon, who later became known as Mennonites. A strong-headed person, Ammann took issue with some of the liberal ways of the Mennonites. He insisted upon returning to the old practices of *Meidung* (shunning), foot washing, and dressing alike. Leading a group of followers, he broke with the main body of the Brethren on March 13, 1694.

Followers of Ammann came to be known as Amish-Mennonites. Because the Amish-Mennonites refust to go to war, they are classified

Meidung

Meidung, or shunning, is a kind of reprimand for breaking church rules. Suppose some church member, a baptized adult, bought an automobile or television or began attending another church. That person would be asked to change his or her ways. If the person refused, then he or she would lose church membership and be shunned.

He or she would not be allowed to eat at the same table as other members of the family, although friends and relatives could talk to the shunned person, hoping to win him or her back to the Amish faith. They could not, however, accept any favors from the shunned one. If the shunned person offered family members or friends a ride, they could not go. On the other hand, friends and family *would* be allowed to offer the shunned person a ride.

as conscientious objectors in the United States, people who do not join the military. During World War II, conscientious objectors had to fill out a card stating their religion. The people at the draft board told the Amish-Mennonites that they could not write down two religious names, so they dropped the name Mennonites and have been known simply as the Amish ever since.

Amish, as well as Mennonites, Brethren, and Hutterites, are Anabaptist. These Protestant faiths baptize adults, not babies, because they do not believe babies are sinful. They also feel a person should be old enough to understand the religious meaning of the baptism rite.

The first Amish lived in an area called the Palatinate, where Switzerland, Germany, and France come together. From the seventeenth cen-

The shaded portion shows the area where the Amish and most Pennsylvania Dutch lived before immigrating to Pennsylvania.

tury until World War II, this land has been the battlefield of Europe.

During the Thirty Years' War (1618–48) Protestant and Catholic armies marched back and forth over this land. The Treaty of Westphalia ended that terrible war, but it said that each prince could decide the official religion of his territory. The prince could choose to be Catholic or Lutheran or Reformed. If the prince chose to be Catholic, then people living in that territory, even those who had attended Lutheran and Reformed churches, had to become Catholic. The Amish refused to join any other church. Many were persecuted and driven from the land.

The *Martyr's Mirror,* found in many Amish homes, records in gory detail how many of the early Christians were tortured by whipping and by cutting off their tongues, hands, feet, and ears, and how they were killed by stoning, burning at the stake, crucifying, and being buried alive.

If that wasn't bad enough, the war and persecutions were followed by famine and disease. People were forced to eat roots, grass, and leaves.

In the War of the Palatinate (1688–97), Louis XIV ordered his generals to destroy the area again. Perhaps it was these horrific experiences of war that cemented the religious conviction of Ammann's followers never to bear arms.

In 1681, William Penn, a member of the Society of Friends, or Quakers, received land in America from King Charles II, who owed a debt to Penn's father. The king named this land Penn Sylvania, or Penn's Woods. Around 1700, Penn traveled up the Rhine through the Palatinate, inviting tormented people to come to Pennsylvania, where he promised religious freedom.

Even though they had suffered greatly, the Amish were not eager to leave their homes. But later, they may have heard that the Menno-

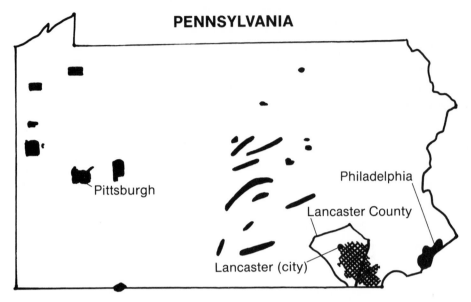

The shaded portions show Amish settlements in Pennsylvania today.

nites who had immigrated to Pennsylvania were prospering and were not mistreated. In any case, on October 8, 1737, the ship *Charming Nancy* arrived in Philadelphia with the first group of Amish. The trip was not pleasant. One passenger wrote that they were "packed into the big boats as closely as herring." He added that the little sailing ship smelled of dysentery and vomit. The food and water were dirty. Lice and sickness were common, and they had to battle terrible storms. No wonder people cursed, and husbands and wives, children and parents fought bitterly.

Most of these new immigrants moved west from Philadelphia and Germantown to what was then the frontier: present-day Berks and Lancaster counties. (Pennsylvania Dutch pronounce the name of the city and county as Lenk-is-ter, not Lan-cast-er, as tourists and other people new to the area want to say.)

Today no Amish remain in Europe. Although there is a small colony reported to be living in South America, the majority of Amish live in Pennsylvania, Ohio, Indiana, Iowa, New York, and Ontario, Canada.

Many of these groups follow slightly different traditions. Some ride in gray buggies, some in black buggies, others in white buggies, and still others in yellow buggies. In some congregations the men wear one suspender (/), while other groups wear crossed pairs (X), others prefer Y-type suspenders, and still others wear H-type. Yet, in spite of these minor differences, their basic beliefs clearly set them apart as Amish.

BACK TO SCHOOL

°○°○°○°○°

After the Bible reading, Anna and the other children line up across the front of the room to sing. The children, arranged from youngest to oldest, stand tall and alert, waiting for Fannie to call out the first song.

Like their mothers and grandmothers, the girls wear long dresses that hang within eight inches of the floor. A little girl, up to eight, wears a pinafore called a *Schlupp Schotzli* over her dress. The older girls wear aprons and capes—which look more like the bib part of an apron.

Some of the older girls wear white prayer caps like their mothers. There is no special time or ceremony for wearing these caps. Anna does not have a cap on now, but all the seventh- and eighth-grade girls are wearing them. Anna does wear a prayer cap for church and other "for good" occasions.

For Amish women, most sweaters are too stylish and too formfitting. However, one might wear a loose black cardigan around the farm, for warmth. Amish never wear jewelry, not even wedding rings. And they wear no makeup, lipstick, or perfume.

This Amish girl is wearing a *Schlupp Schotzli*.

A pair of broadfalls hangs on the line to dry. These pants do not have a "fly." They open with the wide front panel, the broadfall.

Young sons dress like their fathers and grandfathers. Except for their plain colors, their shirts are similar to those anyone else might wear. But their pants have no creases, hip pockets, cuffs, or zippers. They are called "broadfalls" because in place of a fly, there is a large flap that fastens along both sides. Suspenders may just be back in fashion for the "English," but the Amish have been wearing them for many years.

Amos can't wait for spring, when he can kick off his heavy, black, high-topped shoes and go barefoot, even to school. Reuben, a curly headed first grader, is wearing blue sneakers.

The boys will remain clean shaven until they get married. Then they will grow beards but not mustaches.

Why do the Amish dress so plainly, so differently? Some customs —no outer buttons, and beards without mustaches—are reactions to

---

Myth:

Amish wear only drab colors, grays and black.

Truth:

Girls wear dresses and the boys wear shirts of bright colors —teal, royal blue, emerald green, olive green, brown, maroon, taupe, slate blue, mint green, and purple, a favorite color of the Amish. But they don't wear plaids, prints, stripes, or polka dots, just plain, solid colors.

Amish rarely wear red. Certain Western traditions think of red as standing for the devil and lust, and red was the color of the church doors of those who persecuted the Amish when they lived in Europe. Nevertheless, occasionally you might see an Amish girl or woman wearing a red dress.

the uniforms of the Prussian and French army officers who, sporting trim mustaches and chests of brass buttons, waged war through the land of the Amish in the Palatinate.

Sometimes not having things most everyone else has—a certain brand of sneakers or a particular designer sweater—can cause bad feelings among friends. Amish are much more interested in the happiness of one another than in what each is wearing. In fact, wearing the same kind of clothing gives the Amish a sense of belonging. Besides, they think keeping up with the latest fashions is wasteful because often such clothing goes out of style before it is worn out.

∞∞∞

Photographs

It is well known that the Amish do not like to have their pictures taken. Over a hundred years ago Amish bishops worried that some people might admire pictures of themselves, taking pride in how handsome or pretty they looked. So the bishops decided that the Amish should not pose for their pictures.

In respect for the Amish the photographs in this book were purchased from local professional photographers who have lived among the Amish all their lives.

∞∞∞

The Amish see fads and fashions as a conformity to worldliness. They believe in being humble. They do not think one should feel proud of worldly things, such as brand-name jeans or a new skateboard. They also don't believe in feeling proud of God-given talents, such as being smart or good at baseball. They call feeling proud *Hochmut* (hock-moot), taking their inspiration from the Bible, Proverbs 16:18: "Pride leads to destruction and arrogance to downfall."

Therefore, the Amish try to practice *Demut* (day-moot), or humility. 1 Peter 5:5 says: "God resists the proud, but shows favor to the humble."

The children sing a familiar hymn, *"Gott ist die Liebe."* Then they call out numbers of their favorite songs. Reuben wants to sing "This Land Is Your Land."

Whether singing in school, in church, or at Sunday evening "sing-ings," Amish sing in unison. That is, they never sing harmony, or in parts, the way you might in a chorus. However, several of the older boys' voices have changed, forcing them to sing an octave lower than the girls and younger boys. First grader Henry K. strains, squeezing out the notes, sometimes a little off-key but always with great enthusiasm.

The children return to their seats. Then, beginning with the first graders, Fannie goes over math homework. The children not working

"Gott ist die Liebe" is a popular, nonchurch hymn of the Amish.

In this Amish school these "scholars" are reciting their lessons
with an "English" teacher.

with Fannie are busy with their own assignments. There is no talking, no getting out of seats without asking permission.

Occasionally, though, an older girl will leave her seat to help a younger brother or sister. Amish children are taught to care for one another. Older children are expected to look after younger ones. And younger children are expected to listen to their older sisters and brothers.

After math, the children take out their readers. Their reading books are quite old, but not because the Amish cannot afford newer books. They prefer these older editions because they feel these stories do not conflict as much with their way of living as today's books, which reflect modern life-styles.

The first graders parade to the front of the room and read their stories in a monotone that's almost a chant.

What's amazing is that these first graders are bilingual. That means they can speak two languages. Amish children come to school speaking only Pennsylvania Dutch, a dialect of German. They learn to speak English in school, where only English is spoken and read. Every so often, however, Fannie will need to bend over to whisper an explanation in "Dutch" to one of the little first-grade "scholars."

PENNSYLVANIA DUTCH

⚬O⚬O⚬O⚬O⚬

Pennsylvania Dutch has nothing to do with the Netherlands. *Deutsch* means "folk" or "German" in German. The English-speaking settlers in Pennsylvania confused *Deutsch* with Dutch and called all the Pennsylvania Germans "Dutch."

In addition to the Amish, people belonging to the Brethren, Lutheran, Mennonite, Moravian, and Reformed churches are also considered Pennsylvania Dutch. All originally came from the Palatinate area of Europe. At one time many of these people spoke Pennsylvania Dutch, too. Sadly, this dialect of German is dying out. Except for the Amish and some Mennonites, not many people speak Pennsylvania Dutch anymore.

Most Amish speak excellent English, often with a pleasant melody and beat. If you were to speak with an adult over the phone, you might not be able to tell that he or she was Amish.

"Ei, du scheeni" is a popular song in the Pennsylvania Dutch dialect. A *Schnitzelbank* is a cobbler's bench, so the song does not make much sense. But it's fun to sing.

Schnitzelbank

Ei, du scheeni, ei, du scheeni, ei, du scheeni Schnitzelbank.
(Oh, you beautiful, oh, you beautiful, oh, you beautiful cobbler's bench.)
Iss des net en Schnitzelbank? Ya, sell iss en Schnitzelbank.
(Is that not a cobbler's bench? Yes, that is a cobbler's bench.)
Iss des net en kaz und lang (short and long)?
    Ya, sell iss en kaz und lang.
    Kaz und lang, en Schnitzelbank.
Iss des net en gleener Bu (little boy)?
    Ya, sell iss en gleener Bu.
    Gleener Bu, kaz und lang, en Schnitzelbank.
Iss des net en gleener Meedel (little girl)?
    Ya, sell iss en gleener Meedel.
    Gleener Meedel, gleener Bu, kaz und lang, en Schnitzelbank.

The singer can keep adding verses:

En schwazer Schuh (black shoe).
En hesser Boi (hot pie).
En grosser Buch (big book).
En rot Abbel (red apple).
En brau Kuh (brown cow).
En weiss Schof (white sheep).

This billboard advertisement was inspired by the song *"Schnitzelbank."*

I've never heard a Pennsylvania Dutch person say, "Throw me over the fence some hay." However, phrases like this often appear on items sold to tourists.

But you very well may hear Pennsylvania Dutch people say *redd-up* to mean straighten or clean up, as in "You need to *redd-up* your bedroom."

And you might hear someone say, *"Outen* the light," meaning, "Turn off the light." Perhaps that phrase has lasted because the Amish still use gas lamps, which need to be put out.

If you were watering flowers with a hose and you accidently sprayed your friend, he might say, "Don't *spritz* me."

If your hair was messed, you might say it was *strubbly.*

When a young boy or girl just can't seem to sit quietly at the table, the child is said to be *rutchich.* If the child becomes so *rutchich* that he spills the milk, he is called *schusslich.*

A very clumsy person is referred to as *dabbich.*

Can you identify this nursery rhyme?

> *Baa! Baa! Schwarz Schof,*
> *Hoscht du een'che Woll?*
> *O ya! O ya! Drei Seck Voll.*
> *Eener fer der Bauer*
> *Eener fer die Fraa*
> *Eener fer en gleener Bu*
> *Im Haus Newer draa.*

The nursery rhyme is "Baa! Baa! Black Sheep."

THE REST OF
THE SCHOOL DAY

oOoOoOo

Soon Anna's grade forms a line at the front of the room. Each "scholar" takes a turn reading a paragraph. One by one, Fannie asks each a question about reading. Anna's first answer is wrong, and she blushes, embarrassed. Fannie gives her another chance. This time Anna knows the answer, and Fannie flashes a warm smile, as if to say, "Good work!"

The other children working quietly at their seats are exposed to a lot of "review and preview." As the fifth graders recite their lessons, Anna unconsciously receives a review of last year's work, and when the seventh graders give their reports, Anna learns what to expect next year.

When she finishes with her reading homework, Anna begins a letter to her "English" friend. Sylvie is making mobiles to decorate the room. She is coloring a picture of a stag and she has made his nose red!

Hanging under the deer are commandments:

Be Cooperative
Be Honest

Be Kind
Be True
Be Orderly
Be Willing
Be Respectful

Several of these mobiles are already hanging from the ceiling.

For Amish children these phrases are more than words. Like a good Girl Scout or Boy Scout, an Amish child tries to turn these words into deeds. And, in some ways, Amish children have an easier time of it. In this quiet valley, their world has fewer temptations.

Soon it is time for recess. Fannie taps the little bell on her desk. The children put away their books and take out snacks—small bags of popcorn, oranges, apples, corn curls, cookies, or candy. After eating, Anna and the other children sit straight and tall in their seats, awaiting dismissal.

Most Amish have bathrooms in their homes, but there are no lavatories at Amish schools. Instead, two small outhouses stand a reasonable distance from the schoolhouse, one for the boys and the other for the girls.

Outside, the older boys take the sleds propped against the school and race to the knoll that sweeps down to the Beiler farm. Shielded from the sun's direct rays, broad patches of snow survive, scattered about the valley like patterns on a quilt. Near the apple tree the snow is compacted onto the slope. The boys take running starts, then belly flop onto their sleds and sail down the hill so fast their broad-brimmed hats fly off like black saucers tossed to the wind.

Most of the girls stay inside, talking and playing quiet games. A few of the first-grade boys hop around the room. Their hopping, shouting, and laughing become too noisy for Fannie. *"Buwe, geh naus!"* ("Boys, go outside!")

There are no lavatories in Amish schools. Inside is a spigot with cold running water. Outside are outhouses.

Reuben leads the way, grabbing his coat and pulling his black hat over his blond curls. In front of the school where the ground is bare, third- and fourth-grade girls are playing Drop the Hanky. Reuben joins the circle as they hold hands, make a circle, drop their hands, and take a step backward.

The girls drop the hanky behind other girls, ignoring the boys standing nearby. Reuben jumps around, begging the girls to drop the

In winter Amish children like to sled at recess.

hanky behind him. Desperate for attention, Reuben makes up a rhyme that ends with, "I'll take the hanky to scoop the poop." The boys laugh wildly at Reuben's bathroom humor. A few girls giggle but most try very hard to ignore him.

Inside, Sylvie pulls the long cord, ringing the bell perched atop the school, and Reuben marches in, angelic as before.

In school, children are taught to be helpful and cooperative. But they are not encouraged to get better grades than their friends. Rather, by helping one another, they try to do their best work, regardless of what their neighbors can do.

Sometimes classes will compete, however. Near the door is a chart labeled "Did You Remember to Brush Your Teeth Today?" Each of the children in the class with the best record of toothbrushing will get a set of jacks and a ball.

It's important for Amish children to be obedient—to their parents, to their teacher, and to the Amish way of living. They are so obedient that even Amish grown-ups do not know why certain customs are practiced. "That's just the way we do things," Anna's mother says.

Because obedience and cooperation are stressed and competition is not emphasized, there are fewer discipline problems in Amish schools. Children are expected to behave. When a "scholar" does misbehave, the teacher will first speak to him or her. If the problem is serious, the child might have to stay in at recess. Only for very serious misbehavior, such as lying, cheating, or swearing, might a "scholar" be spanked. Like most good teachers, Fannie prefers using encouragement and rewards rather than punishment.

Quietly, the children take their seats and get out their English workbooks. Today they are working on homophones. Many of the girls and

This young "scholar" is doing her seatwork while children in another grade recite their lessons.

several of the boys take pride in their handwriting, carefully shaping each letter as they write words in their workbooks.

Before lunch the children have fun with "bees." The fifth and sixth graders are drilled on state capitals. Standing in a line at the front of the room, "scholars" who get the answer right move past a neighbor, toward the beginning of the line. They move back if the answer is wrong. Anna almost lands at the end of the line, but when asked to name the capitals of New Jersey and Massachusetts, she answers, "Trenton" and "Boston," and ends up somewhere in the middle. The seventh and eighth graders have a more difficult bee. They are quizzed on capitals of European countries.

Then each grade takes part in a math bee. The little "scholars" practice their addition and subtraction tables. Third and fourth graders are expected to know their times tables. But by the time the sixth graders are in line, Fannie is calling out much harder problems.

"Twelve times three, minus eight, divided by four, times seven, plus five, divided by nine."

Without a moment's delay, the children fire answers like a machine gun: "Seven. Six. Eight. Six. Five. Six. Six." All except quiet Anna, who seems to want to speak just as the last of the other children shout their answers.

Fannie notices Anna and gives her a problem she has a chance of getting right. Anna looks toward the ceiling, then she calls out an answer too quickly. She shakes her head and changes her answer. But that is wrong, too. Fannie says, "Let's try another one." She says another problem more slowly. This time Anna gets it right. Her face brightens. Fannie smiles, too.

After the seventh and eighth graders take their turns at math, Fannie taps the bell on her desk. It's lunchtime.

There is no cafeteria in this school. All the children and Fannie carry their own lunches. They fetch their brightly colored lunch boxes from the shelf in the mudroom. Some of the yellow, red, and blue plastic lunch boxes are decorated with cartoons such as Strawberry Shortcake and *Return of the Jedi*. Only a few children have old-style black-metal lunch pails.

The boisterous talk and laughter, the banging and clanging of cafeteria trays typical of most elementary and middle schools is absent. The only sounds are the clicking of lunch-box latches and the crackling of plastic wrap as the children take out their Lebanon bologna sandwiches, or the snapping of someone biting into a firm apple or breaking a hard pretzel. Listening closely, you can probably hear the children pouring milk from their bright plastic thermoses. Saved for last is a treat—cookies, cake, or maybe a slice of snitz pie.

During the lunch recess the first- and second-grade boys play with their toy cars. "My hippy hot rod can really go," Reuben says, shooting his miniature car the length of the classroom.

The older boys get up a game of *Mosch Balle,* or Corner Ball. Behind the school where the schoolyard is flat and free of snow, Aaron, one of the seventh-grade boys, lays out four bases, almost like a baseball diamond. Then he and Jake pick sides.

Jake's side is "in." Jake and Sam stand inside the box. Aaron and three of his players stand on the bases. Aaron has the ball, about the size of a baseball with a leather covering, but soft like a Hacky Sack ball.

Aaron takes the ball and fires at Amos. He skips, but the ball clips his left foot. Amos is out and another team member takes his place.

One of Aaron's players, John, throws at Sam, but Sam ducks and the ball goes sailing over to the fence. So John is out, and he is replaced by another player, Steve.

The game continues with the boys shouting in Dutch. *"Geb acht!"* ("Watch out!") *"Guck datt hie!"* ("Look there!") But when Amos asks Aaron, *"Was hoscht du?"* ("What have you?") Aaron tells him the score in English, "Eight to six."

Meanwhile, some of the younger boys are sledding, while the first-grade boys have joined the girls, first through eighth grades, who are playing Big Bad Wolf. Lydia is "it" and must hide while the other girls count, "One o'clock, two o'clock, three o'clock . . ." By the time they shout, "The old gray wolf must be gone," Lydia has hidden and tries to sneak up and tag them before they reach the safety of "home," the school door.

It's down to Steve and Aaron on the bases and Eli, who's "in." Ringing the box, the other boys cheer wildly. Steve and Aaron run from base to base, tossing the ball back and forth, getting it "hot." Just when they have Eli dizzy, running this way and that, Steve uncorks a hard throw, nicking him in the back just as the bell rings.

With all that running, the children are thirsty. After hanging up their coats and hats, they crowd around the sink to get drinks. There is no water fountain in this Amish school. On pegs above the sink hang thirty-seven cups, one for each of the children, plus Fannie.

Fannie begins the afternoon by reading aloud *Little House on the Prairie.* Later, when she is helping one grade, children in the other grades take out books from their desks. A small collection of books stands neatly in a small bookcase under a bulletin board.

Amish children like good stories, especially horse stories, such as *King of the Wind.* But they do not read stories about magic. Stories with magic imply that events do not occur by the will of God, and Amish believe that everything happens by the hand of God.

Anna puts down her fancy pen and carefully folds her letter to Elizabeth, laying it beside the picture of a horse she drew.

Setting the letter and picture aside, Anna opens *Black Beauty.* A purple-and-white bookmark she made out of yarn marks the place where she stopped reading. Anna is pleased with her bookmark and fancy pen. Of course, she would never think of bragging about them. As long as decorated lunch boxes, fancy pens, pretty bookmarks, and toy cars do not disrupt the love among the children, no one takes notice.

At day's end, Fannie checks the children's desks. Anna has carefully arranged her books and things. Orderliness is important to the Amish, from their farms, barns, gardens, and homes to children's school desks. But Reuben's desk is a mess! Papers are stuffed here, books shoved in there. More papers and little knobby pencils spill onto the floor. "*Ei yi, yi,* Reuben. *Redd-up* your desk at once," Fannie says. Reuben blushes, smiles, and sets to work.

HOME

◦O◦O◦O◦

Stepping from the school bus, Anna opens the mailbox, takes out the mail, and hands it to Amos. Then she lays her letter to Elizabeth inside the cavernous box, shuts the lid, and raises the flag so the letter carrier knows to stop. Thumbing through the mail, Amos finds a catalogue of workhorses. He leafs through the magazines as he walks slowly down the lane.

Anna says, *"Mache schnell!"* ("Make quickly!" or "Hurry up!") to her sisters and brother. She knows there are chores to be done.

Amish children begin helping around the house and farm as early as four years of age, and by the age of six, they assume some responsibility. But they do not look upon these chores as hard work, as something to be dreaded or avoided. In fact, they actually look forward to their chores. Anna says her favorite "happy time" activity is feeding the chickens and collecting the eggs.

After changing from her pretty blue dress to her brown "working dress" with its black apron, she dashes for the henhouse. Her little brother and sisters follow close behind. They want to see if the chicks have been delivered.

Even before opening the door, she can hear their high-pitched peep, peep, peeping. "Ooooh!" Anna says when she sees the little yellow bundles of down scurrying around the pen. She lifts one out and gives it to her little brother to hold.

"Ouch!" he says after it pecks him.

"Mustn't hold it too tight," Anna says, showing him how to handle the chicks gently.

Anna laughs as some of the chicks suddenly fall asleep. She raps the cage and they all scurry around, peeping loudly, until a few close their eyes again.

But when Anna begins pouring feed, the chicks crowd the trays, even stepping on one another in their rush to eat.

At the other end of the chicken house, Barred Rock hens cluck and scratch. There Anna collects big brown eggs. Accidentally, she drops one. Splat! *"Dunnerwetter!"* she says. *"Des macht mich bees!"* ("Thunder-weather! That makes me mad.")

After putting the eggs in the cool cellar, Anna and her sisters help Mamm set the table. Pot pie is cooking on the gas stove. But along the countertop in the big kitchen you will see no electric mixers, food processors, microwave ovens, or other electric appliances. Even in the kitchen, effort and time make up for convenience, speed, ease, and comfort. Things are just done the old way.

While the children are in school, Amish eat their big cooked meal for supper in the evening. Come spring, when school is out, Mamm will serve the big dinner meal at noon, and they will have soup and sandwiches for supper.

Anna's favorite foods are homemade pizza and ice cream, and she also likes stopping at the pizza shop and ice cream parlor when she goes to town with Mamm and Daat.

<hr/>

Myth:
The Amish have seven sweets and seven sours with every meal.

Truth:
The only place you'll be served seven sweets and seven sours is in some tourist restaurants.

<hr/>

AMISH FOODS

oOoOoOo

Many Amish foods tend to be plain, often heavy in carbohydrates. But the Amish enjoy some unique and tasty dishes.

Dandelion. In the spring before the dandelions' distinctive yellow flowers have bloomed, Amish children dig out the dandelion plants. In the kitchen, children cut off the roots, then wash and separate the green leaves. Like any salad, what makes dandelions so special is the dressing.

Dandelion salad dressing is made by first frying bacon. Make a gravy from the bacon fat by adding a tablespoon of flour and heating it until it's brown. Then stir in one cup of milk. Boil, then add one tablespoon each of salt and sugar and vinegar. Finally, slice hard-boiled eggs into the salad and sprinkle bacon bits into the sauce. Add the sauce to the dandelion greens before serving.

Snitz un Knepp. Snitz is dried slices of sweet apples. *Knepp* is something like a dumpling. The *Snitz* is soaked in water overnight. The next day brown sugar is added and this mixture is cooked. Then the dumplings, or *Knepp,* are dropped into the boiling snitz and cooked like doughnuts. *Snitz un Knepp,* often with small slices of ham added, is served like a stew.

Snitz pie is a delicious pie made from dried apples.

Chow-chow is actually pickled vegetables: celery, kidney beans, cauliflower, carrots, and string beans.

Cup cheese is a creamy, smooth cheese that's spread on bread or crackers. Known only in Lancaster County, cup cheese is made by slowly cooking the curds from cottage cheese.

Lebanon bologna is a type of cold sausage. It is maroon in color and flecked with white dots of fat. It has a peppery, smoked taste.

Red beets is a redundancy, since all beets are red. To anyone else they are simply beets or sugar beets.

Red beet eggs are pickled eggs. Hard-boiled eggs are allowed to soak overnight in a large jar of red beets and vinegar. As you might expect, the white parts of these eggs take on a reddish color (the yolks remain yellow) and have the mild, sweet-sour taste of pickled beets. Many Easter eggs become red beet eggs on Easter Monday.

When Daat bows his head, everyone silently says a prayer. Anna says,

> *"Spiess, Gott, Trinke, Gott,*
> *Alle armind Kinder die auf Erden sind."*

> *"All the poor children of the world*
> *should receive food and drink."*

Following the moment of silence, Daat says, *"Helfet eich selwert"* ("Help yourselves"). Mamm helps the little ones, dishing out servings

Myth: The Amish paint hex signs on their barns.

Hex signs appear on some Pennsylvania Dutch barns, and their beautiful designs have become symbols of the Pennsylvania Dutch. Folklorists believe that they were once thought to keep witches away from the innocent barnyard animals. But Amish do not believe in witches because witches represent anti-Christian beliefs. That is, as servants of the devil who perform magic and evil, witches stand for values opposite the goodness of Christ. So you won't find hex signs on any Amish barns.

Truth:

Today, any hex signs you see on the sides of barns are just for fancy and are not Amish.

of chicken pot pie—pieces of boiled chicken mixed with potatoes and covered with dough squares. There is little talking, no idle conversation, as the other children help themselves. But dinner often becomes a family meeting time.

Levi says, "I hear Anna is allowed to visit her 'English' friend."

Daat and Mamm wait, knowing Levi has more to say.

"The rest of us don't have an 'English' friend."

Daat takes a few moments to think, to understand Levi's complaint. Then he says, "What do you think, Mamm?"

"Maybe Anna's friend could take all of you somewhere close by, perhaps?" she suggests, dishing out a small portion of cole slaw for Anna's youngest sister.

Obediently, Anna accepts the family's decision.

For a while it is quiet until Anna's youngest brother belches. But no one makes a fuss. Amish do not think it is improper to belch at the table.

When everyone is finished eating, they all remain seated for a silent prayer. Then Daat gets up and hurries to the barn. Soon Levi and his brothers follow.

Anna and her sisters scoot around the kitchen, helping Mamm clear the table and wash the dishes before heading to the barn, where Daat and the boys are already hard at work feeding the cows.

EVENING

◦○◦○◦○◦

Morning and evening, seven days a week, Anna and her sisters help Mamm with the milking. Sometimes it gets boring.

"Let's race!" Anna says to her sister.

"Okay," Rebecca says, eager for the challenge.

Quickly, Anna wipes Brownie's four teats and pulls a small amount of milk from each before attaching the cups. Once fastened, the cups bounce up and down, sucking milk from the cow to send it up through transparent plastic tubes. Anna watches the air bubbles dance through the hoses to the stainless-steel buckets. She and her brothers must lug these buckets full of milk to the bulk-storage tank in the little room attached to the barn. There the milk is kept cool until the eighteen-wheel truck comes to take it to the dairy.

"I win!" Rebecca shouts victoriously from across the barn.

"You're ahead, two to one," Anna says, not at all disappointed she lost.

Finished with Brownie, Anna moves on to Spotty. But just as she attaches the first cup, Spotty kicks and Anna jumps back. Working around large animals, Anna knows to stay alert. Mamm rushes over and holds Spotty's tail high in the air so Anna can fasten all the cups.

But she'll leave Boots for Daat. That's the name Anna gave to cow number forty-five because of the black markings around her feet. Although all the cows have identification tags pinched to their ears, Anna knows all forty-six cows by name. Ever since this once-gentle heifer had her first calf, Boots has been ornery at milking time. She misses her calf, which was taken from her and given formula so the cow's milk could be sold to the dairy.

Mamm screws a brace around Boots's hips. This device restricts her kicking. Then Daat straps her fast to the railing so she can't jostle. Finally, Levi holds her tail up high. But just as Daat hooks up one set of cups, she somehow manages to kick, anyway, knocking them off. Daat tightens the strap, Levi holds the tail higher, and they try again. This time Boots behaves, maybe because she has no choice.

Having fed the cows, Levi helps his younger brother feed the horses. Skip and Blaze, the two standardbreds, are kept in stalls behind the cows. Here, deep within the barn, it is dark. Years of cobwebs decorate the beams with misty lace. Levi hangs his lantern on a post, takes a pitchfork, and removes the old straw. After cutting the binder twine, he breaks apart a new bale, spreading the fresh straw around the stall. These two spirited driving horses, used mostly for pulling buggies, neigh and nod their heads as Levi and Amos give them fresh water and oats.

Levi wishes Daat would give him a colt. "Someday soon," his father keeps promising. Levi takes good care of the standardbreds to show Daat just how well he would take care of one of his own.

Enough dreaming. The Belgians need to be fed, too. These six gentle giants, Bob, Jim, Betsy, Rock, Jerry, and Charlie, each weighing a ton and standing about seventeen hands, or more than five feet high at the withers, do the fieldwork: plowing, mowing, and baling.

Anna has the big responsibility of cleaning the milkers. To prevent contamination she rinses them and the hoses in a vat containing sterilizing solution. As important as this job is, it is not one of Anna's favorites.

With the evening chores completed, Mamm sets out a shoofly pie along with some thinly sliced bologna and cheese, orange drink for the children, and strong black coffee for Daat.

Shoofly pie is a pie made mostly of molasses. The name, so the story goes, came when the women set these pies on the windowsill to cool. The sweetness of the pies attracted flies, which the women chased away, with a "Shoo, fly!"

Here's a recipe for shoofly pie. Because you must bake the pie in a hot oven, make it only when an adult can help.

Wet Bottom Shoofly Pie

One unbaked 9-inch pie shell
Crumbs:
    1½ cups flour
    ½ cup brown sugar
    2 tablespoons lard (shortening)

Combine the flour, brown sugar, and lard in a bowl and cut with a pastry knife or rub with your fingers until the dough forms fine crumbs.

Bottom:

    1 teaspoon soda

    1 cup boiling water

    ½ cup King (corn) syrup

    ½ cup baking molasses

    ¼ teaspoon salt

    1 egg

Dissolve the soda in the boiling water in a bowl. Add the King syrup, molasses, and salt, and stir well. Pour ⅓ of this liquid into the 9-inch pie crust. Sprinkle ⅓ crumb mixture over liquid. Pour in another ⅓ liquid topped with ⅓ of the crumbs, followed by final ⅓ liquid and remaining ⅓ crumbs.

Bake at 375 degrees for ten minutes, then bake at 350 degrees for 30 minutes.
Top with vanilla ice cream.

"Des is gut," Daat says, brushing a few crumbs from his beard.

At the far end of the large kitchen he lights the gas lamp and sits in the rocker to read the *Budget.* This Amish newspaper reports births, deaths, who visited whom, and news about crops.

Because Amish children have farm chores, they do not have homework. All assignments are completed while the teacher works with the other grades. So, until bedtime, Anna and her brothers and sisters can relax. But there's no television to watch! Of course, that means no VCRs or video games. And no phones to call friends.

Mamm teaches Anna how to play "Oh, Susannah" on her new harmonica. Mamm plays a few bars, then Anna imitates. After some practice, Anna learns the tune as Mamm sings along. While her younger brother and sisters play a game of marbles on the floor, Levi is reading a novel, *The Black Stallion.*

Later in the evening Grossdawdi (Grandpa) and Grossmudder (Grandmother) stop over. Amish grandparents do not live in senior citizen's homes. Instead, they live in the *Grossdawdi Haus,* which is simply an addition to Anna's family's house. They like to visit, and whenever there are big jobs to be done, like canning time in August, Grossmudder is always there to help. Mostly she and Grossdawdi keep to themselves. Sometimes Anna does not see Grossmudder for several days in a row.

This evening Grossmudder wants to work a little on the quilt she and Mamm are stitching. Sometimes they make quilts to sell. But this quilt is for Anna's youngest sister.

Levi's ears perk up but he keeps his eyes on his book when Grossdawdi and Daat talk about looking for another horse.

Before bedtime, Mamm reads *Least of All* to Anna's younger sisters and brother.

Soon all the children file upstairs, except Levi, who takes his time. After they change into their nightclothes, Mamm says, *"Graddle nie,"* ("Crawl in") and tucks them in bed.

CHURCH

◦C◦C◦C◦C◦

Sundays are busy days for Anna and her family. Every other Sunday they attend church. Although there are some "church" Amish, Old Order Amish conduct their services in the homes of the members. In just about every Amish home, folding doors between the dining and living area and the sitting room open to make an extra-large room, big enough to hold church. This Sunday church is at Daniel Esh's place.

On Saturday Mamm helps Alvina Esh bake snitz pies. Daat helps Daniel collect extra benches, which they arrange in rows. Levi helps Daniel's son Ben carry out manure and put down fresh straw so visiting horses have a clean stable.

That evening Anna presses her prayer cap with an iron she heats on the stove. Mamm trims the boys' hair, taking care to make sure the bangs are straight and keeping the back even with the middle of their ears. But she doesn't put a bowl over their heads to do this. That's another good tale for tourists.

On church Sundays the family awakens at the same time as on weekdays. There's no "sleeping in" on an Amish farm, although some mornings Anna wishes, just once, she could stay in bed.

But cows don't know it's Sunday and must be milked. Chickens don't know it's the weekend and must be fed. Eggs must still be gathered. So it's out to the barn. Everyone pitches in with the chores.

Levi works quickly. He wants to finish so he can hitch Skip to the buggy.

With the chores completed, the family changes into church clothing. Daat and the boys are wearing white shirts with black vests, black pants and coats. Teenage Levi is wearing a black hat with a crease to flatten the crown, while Daat and the younger boys, Amos and David, wear black hats with curved crowns. Daat wears an overcoat with a cape; Levi has just begun wearing a *Mutzi,* which is a frock coat with rounded edges in front and a slit at the bottom in back and a rounded standing collar. It is fastened not with buttons but with hooks and eyes.

The girls wear white capes and aprons fastened with straight pins to their colored dresses. Mamm is wearing a black cape over a royal blue dress with a "for good" black apron. Little Sarah wears her *Schlupp Schotzli* over her purple dress. Mamm and each of the girls are wearing black stockings and black shoes that tie. Rebecca and Sarah are wearing pretty blue bonnets, while Mamm's and Anna's bonnets are black. Because it is so cold, Mamm and the girls have on homemade coats underneath their black shawls.

Daat and Mamm sit in the front with Anna's little brother snuggled in between. It's so cold you can see Skip's breath streaming from his nostrils, and even though the buggy is enclosed with a windshield and side doors, there's no heater. To keep warm, Daat and Mamm cover

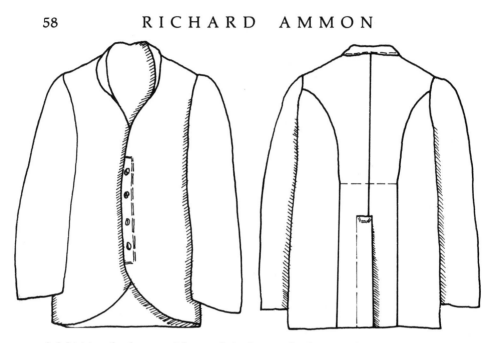

A *Mutzi* is a frock coat with rounded edges in the front, a slit at the bottom in the back, and a rounded standing collar. It does not have buttons but is fastened with hooks and eyes.

their legs with the horse blanket, which is really for keeping horse hairs off their clothing. The rest of the children bundle in blankets in the rear of the buggy.

With his head held high, Skip prances down the long dirt lane to the paved country road. It's five miles to Daniel Esh's farm.

Some "Englishers" think the idea of riding in a buggy is romantic, but this short trip, which takes about five minutes by car, will take Anna's family about half an hour. Twenty miles, which takes between an hour to an hour and a half, is about as far as a horse can travel without resting.

There is also the constant fear of cars, which is why buggies are now equipped with headlamps and flashing rear lights. Even careful drivers can unexpectedly come upon a slow-moving buggy traveling around a bend or over the crest of a hill.

Mostly, "Englishers" and Amish cooperate. It's not unusual to see a long line of patient traffic backed up, waiting turns to pass a buggy. Often, as soon as they can, the Amish pull off to the side of the road, allowing cars to pass safely.

Turning into Esh's lane, Daat pulls back on the reins, slowing the proud horse, as they take their place in the line of buggies going to service. When Daat stops by the house, Mamm, Anna, and her sisters get out and go inside. As Daat and the boys park the buggy near the barnyard, they are met by Daniel's sons, who unhitch Skip and take him into the barn.

In the barn the men gather in small groups, greeting one another. The muted talk is accompanied by warm handshakes. When the preachers quietly leave for the house, that is the signal to begin the ritual order for entering the service. After hanging their coats on harness hooks in the barn, for there are usually no closets in Amish homes, the ministers go first, followed by the oldest men. The middle-aged men enter at a leisurely pace. Lingering until the last possible moment, the unmarried boys file in, oldest to youngest.

The women and girls assemble in the kitchen. After hanging their coats, bonnets, and shawls in the washhouse or woodshed, the women and girls enter after the men but before the boys. Preschool boys sit with their fathers; preschool girls sit with their mothers.

The service may last three hours! And it's all conducted in German, beginning with the hymns, which are sung a capella (unaccompanied) and ever so slowly. The *Vorsinger,* or song leader, usually an elderly man but never officially appointed, announces the hymn found in the *Ausbund,* or hymnal.

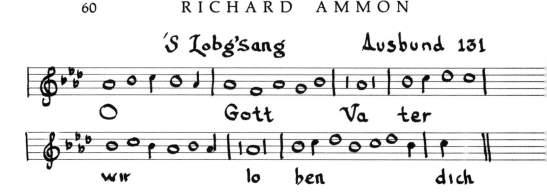

" 'S Lobg'sang" is an Amish hymn. Like all hymns sung in church, it is sung very slowly.

The 140 hymns come from Gregorian chants, the very early, single-melody music without harmony sung by monks. The *Ausbund* contains no music, just the words to these sorrowful hymns, which praise the sufferings of the Anabaptists and Christians of long ago.

From memory, the *Vorsinger* begins singing what appears to be a solo, but after the first syllable, which may last several beats, the rest of the congregation joins in. The singing of one hymn may last twenty to thirty minutes!

After the *Anfang,* or introductory sermon, there is a prayer, followed by the reading of a chapter from the Bible. As the preacher begins the *Es schwere Deel,* or main sermon, a mother carries her sleeping baby upstairs, laying it on a bed with two other babies. Two mothers go to the kitchen to nurse their infants.

Anna's little brother plays with Mamm's handkerchief, making little puppet animals. There's no Sunday school for children, and they are expected to behave during the service. They may entertain themselves as long as they do not disturb the grown-ups.

A congregation may have several ministers. Just as teachers receive no formal training, neither do the preachers. In fact, they are chosen by lot. When a new one is needed, baptized men and women suggest men they believe would be good at preaching. A slip of paper is placed in one *Ausbund*. Then each nominated man takes an *Ausbund* from a stack. The man who finds a slip of paper in his *Ausbund* becomes the new minister. Like many other Amish practices, it is unthinkable to refuse what the Amish feel is the will of God.

Foot Washing

Twice a year, Easter and October, after the Sacrament of Communion, church members (baptized adults) bring towels and buckets of water into church for foot washing, to commemorate Jesus' washing of his disciples' feet. John 13:14:

> *If I then, your Lord and Teacher, have washed your feet, you also ought to wash one another's feet.*

While singing a hymn two men at a time come forward. The younger of the two stoops, as a sign of humility, and washes the others feet. Pairs of women also wash each other's feet. After they finish, they clasp hands and kiss each other as a symbol of love and fellowship. Then the oldest says, *"Da Herr sei mit uns,"* ("the Lord be with us") and the other replies, *"Amen, sum Frieda"* ("Amen, in peace").

The preacher dabs his forehead as he vigorously compares a story from the Old Testament to one from the New Testament. But there still remains over an hour of sitting, and the backless benches become harder and harder. When he finally concludes by reading another chapter from the Bible and sits down, other ministers sitting in the congregation deliver brief "testimonies," or *Zeugnis,* to the main sermon.

Unlike many religions, Amish do not try to get people to join their church. But anyone is free to join just so long as he or she is willing to obey all the rules.

Following the closing remarks, everyone kneels while the ministers read a prayer. All rise for the benediction, and as the ministers say, *"Jesum Christum,"* the congregation genuflects. This unison bending of the knees symbolizes obedience, reverence, and unity. After announcements and the singing of the closing hymn, they leave in the reverse order of their entrance, with the little ones going out first.

Now the men clear away some of the benches and the women and girls hustle about, setting the tables with pies, homemade bread, butter, and jams, cheese, pickles, Lebanon bologna, and coffee. This light

On summer Sunday evenings Amish teenagers often gather to play volleyball.

meal is not intended to be a banquet, just a little something to eat until they get home that evening.

In the afternoon the men and women talk and the children play. Anna is related in some way to most everyone. Among the families, she has twenty-six aunts and uncles and more first cousins than she can count. These extended families of aunts, uncles, grandparents, and cousins bring to the Amish a sense of strength and belonging. No one is allowed to feel left out.

By four o'clock, it is time to return home to milk the cows.

That evening Levi and Eli Lapp return for a "singing" to the home where church was held. This is a time for teenagers to get together to have fun and get to know one another.

Soon, maybe, Daat will give Levi his own horse and an open buggy so he can go *rum springa* (running around). Amish teenagers are not much different from "English" teens. Some Amish boys have decorated their buggies with distinctive mirrors, reflectors, and other gadgets. Some Amish teens belong to gangs that "hang out" together to do many of the same things as "English" teens do.

During this time, some teens may engage in some "worldly" activities, such as sneaking into a movie or drinking. Once they become baptized, though, they give up such foolishness.

Mostly, in these valleys, Amish teens gather in someone's home for a singing. In the summer they may first play volleyball before going to the barn to sing.

SUNDAYS WHEN THEY DON'T HAVE CHURCH

◦O◦O◦O◦O◦

There is no church service every other Sunday. After the morning chores, Mamm reads Bible stories, in English and in German, to Anna's sisters and brothers. Anna and Levi read their own books. Even Daat is reading a novel Levi recommended—*Hatchet.*

Mamm expects visitors on those Sundays, which Anna calls "the Sundays when we don't have church." Anna and Rebecca help Mamm clean the house and bake cookies and pies for friends and relatives who may stop by to visit.

Daat thinks about hitching up Skip. "Maybe we'll stop by and see how Abner's sows are coming along." But if Abner isn't home, Daat will drive the buggy to another brother or cousin until he finds someone to visit.

"Daat," Anna says, "someone's coming." At the far end of the lane there's a small figure carrying something brightly colored. Earlier that morning Anna noticed the gray station wagon parked at the house across the road from the pasture. She knew her "English" friend, Elizabeth, had come to visit her grandmother.

In the kitchen, Anna gives Elizabeth a valentine she's made. It's a big red heart trimmed with white lace. On the outside Anna wrote, "For My Friend." Opening the card, Elizabeth reads, "Will You Be My Valentine?" Then Elizabeth gives Anna a valentine, a fancy one she cut from red-and-white paper. Because Elizabeth has come, visiting Abner can wait until another day.

At milking time, Anna takes Elizabeth along into the barn. After Anna finishes her chores, the girls give the newborn calves their bottles of formula. It's as if the heifers are racing to see which can empty its bottle first.

Afterward Elizabeth and Anna have a snack of bachelor hats and milk and play Mennonite Manners with Rebecca.

Here's how to make bachelor hats. On a Ritz cracker, spread some peanut butter and top it off with a marshmallow.

Place it in the broiler until the marshmallow is lightly toasted.

To play Mennonite Manners, Anna rolls a pair of dice, trying to get "doubles." While she rolls the dice, Elizabeth and Rebecca quickly write numbers on a pad to see who can reach one hundred first before Anna throws doubles. Each of the girls takes several turns throwing dice before Rebecca calls out, "I win!"

No one knows how this game got its name, especially since the children are not particularly "mannerly" when they snatch the paper and pencil and dice from one another.

SPRING

∘C∘C∘C∘C∘

Although the patches of snow have vanished, the trees remain bare and the lawn and pasture keep their winter brown. Only the purple and gold crocuses along the walk brighten the mud season, that transition between winter and spring, when unpaved roads, gardens, and fields ooze with wet, thick, brown earth.

It is a time of waiting. Oaks and maples brimming with buds wait for warmer days before bursting into leaf. Farmers wait for their fields to dry before beginning spring plowing.

But Anna can't wait. In school the boys and girls, preparing for Easter, exchange names. Anna picks Susie B. In the evening she decorates a brown egg, painting pretty flowers, designs, and Susie's name on it. In school on the Thursday before Good Friday, Fannie calls out family names—Beiler, Esh, Stoltzfus. . . . When their last name is called, Anna and her sisters and brother rush outside and hide their decorated eggs. Once all the eggs are hidden, the children go outside, each to find the egg with his or her name. Children dash this way and that, laughing and shouting. Anna is among the last to find her egg, a white one with a red tulip.

There's no school Easter Monday. From the kitchen window, Anna watches for Elizabeth. After dinner, or what "Englishers" call lunch, she sees her walking down the lane, carrying a small bag and something red.

Anna puts on her shawl and bonnet and hurries out the door. The sun streams through the clouds as a southwesterly breeze kicks up some oak leaves, sending them scurrying across the yard like little scampering mice.

Running down the lane, Anna meets Elizabeth below the grove. They talk for a few minutes, then crawl through the barbed-wire fence and start walking across the pasture. The cows, out for a little exercise on this early-spring afternoon, don't seem to mind.

Inside, Anna's brothers and sisters crowd around the window. They see Elizabeth and Anna looking eastward. They look, too, out beyond the trees at the fence row. Then they put on their coats and dash to the pasture. Levi, absorbed in his book, doesn't pay any attention. But Daat peeks out the window, then joins the children. Even Mamm goes outside. Way up in the sky, far beyond the small woods, sails a red kite with a long tail of colorful streamers.

It isn't long until Levi also goes to see what all the excitement is about. Anna gives him the string and spool and lets him fly the kite for a while. Throughout the afternoon friends and relatives stop by to visit and watch the kite, now a single red polka dot in a blue sky. When the breeze dies, the kite slowly drifts to a soft landing in the field, and everyone returns to the house.

The two girls haven't seen each other since Valentine's Day. Inside, Elizabeth opens the bag and offers everyone chocolate-covered peanut-butter eggs she and her mother made for Easter.

An Amish boy plows the fields in the spring. It takes about four times as long to plow with horses as it does by tractor. Therefore, Amish keep their farms small and manageable, about eighty acres.

As pleasant as springtime is, to the farmer it means dawn-to-dusk work once the soil has dried. Every day as soon as school lets out, Amos hitches up a team and heads for the fields. Starting in the back field, Amos throws the lever that sets the two plows into the earth. He gives the reins a shake, and Jerry and Charlie, the pair of gentle Belgians, lurch forward. Twisting like soft chocolate ice cream squeezed from the custard machine, the stubbled field curls over in long ribbons of deep, rich soil. Each season seems to have distinct odors, and Amos takes pleasure in drawing a deep breath, savoring the aroma of freshly tilled earth.

Slowly, at a walking pace, Jerry and Charlie lumber down one row and up another. Peering across the valley, Amos sees his "English" neighbor in his powerful tractor pulling eight plows that will cultivate in a few hours what will take Amos all day.

After two hours, it is time for supper and milking. It is also time to change the team of horses. Once the cows are fed, Amos hitches up Bob and Rock and heads back into the field. Daat and Levi would work all night if they could. They want to plow and disk as much as they can before the next spring rain. After a rain they must wait for the fields to dry before working the soil again.

Day after day, row after row, they plow over eighty acres in all. Plowing, disking, planting. First the corn, over sixty acres, which will become feed for the cows and horses. Then the peppers, the cash crop.

During the winter, Daat, his brother, and their father built a farm implement for laying the black plastic that looks like a long roll of a continuous garbage bag. This covering keeps the pepper plants from being overgrown with weeds. But, unlike the corn, which is planted by machine, peppers must be set in the ground by hand, one at a time. It's hard work, but not as backbreaking as picking them later in the early autumn.

One afternoon, on a Sunday when they don't have church, Daat and Levi hike up into the woods to check the springhouse and reservoir tank for any leaks. They walk up through the orchard so white with blossoms that, when the wind blows, it looks as if it is snowing.

In many Amish communities, windmills punctuate the landscape

Windmills, used to pump water from wells, dot the Pennsylvania Dutch landscape.

like upside-down exclamation points. Because Amish do not use electric pumps, these windmills are used to lift water from their wells. But in this valley many families get water from springs located up on the sides of the mountains. Gravity, or the force of water naturally flowing downhill, provides plenty of water pressure for their plumbing.

Daat and Levi can find no leaks, even with the springhouse and tank so full a steady stream gushes from the overflow spout.

Soon after Anna sees the gray station wagon pull into the driveway across the road, she cuts across the pasture to Elizabeth's grandmother's house. "Daat wants to talk to his brother Abner about buying another driving horse. Want to come along?" Anna asks.

"Sure," Elizabeth says, always ready to take a buggy ride.

Daat starts up the lane, stopping to let the girls hop onto the back of the spring wagon. The ride is bumpier and bouncier than in a car, but it is slower, too, allowing riders to notice things along the way. Two bluebirds fly from their little house on a fence post, a sure sign of spring.

Farther down the lane, Elizabeth sees a cow lying in the soft grass of the grove, far from the other grazing holsteins. "Why's that cow all alone?" Elizabeth asks.

"That's Ava. She's probably going to have a calf," Anna tells her, matter-of-factly. Because cows produce milk only after they've had a calf, there are frequent births around a dairy farm.

At Abner's the men agree to look at some driving horses to pull the buggies, after spring plowing and planting.

On their return down the lane, Anna and Elizabeth see Ava licking her newborn, cleaning the afterbirth. Daat jumps off the wagon and examines the new calf. As Daat climbs back into his seat Anna asks, "Can we keep her?"

"Yah, it's a heifer."

Farming is a business. Daat cannot afford to keep male cattle, who produce no milk. They are sold quickly. Only females, called heifers, are kept. In about two years, Ava's calf will bear her own calf and start giving milk.

Ava's calf is standing now. But Ava is lying down again. "I think she's going to have twins!" Anna exclaims. The girls watch for a while, but having a calf takes some time, and Elizabeth must go to her grandmother and Anna must help with the milking.

Anna walks partway up the lane with Elizabeth. On the way they see wildflowers—buttercups, dandelions, spring beauties, and jack-in-the-pulpits. "Spring is here," Anna says.

SCHOOL PICNIC

o0o0o0o0o

Because Amish children are needed around the farm in the spring, the school year ends in early May. State law requires Amish children to attend school the same number of days as "English" children, so in order to finish early, Amish children have fewer vacations. They go to school between Christmas and New Year's Day. There's no long Easter vacation. They have off only on Good Friday and Easter Monday. And it has to be a mighty powerful snowstorm to keep some father from hitching up a sleigh to take all the Amish children to school when school buses are not running.

One special day during the last week of school, the children are a little more excited than usual. This day they sing a few more songs, and instead of opening books for reading, writing, and arithmetic, they recite poems they've been memorizing.

Pretty soon necks stretch to see out the windows. A parade of buggies pulls into the school yard. Mothers and fathers, brothers and sisters already out of school and those too young have come for the school picnic.

Busily, the women and girls unpack picnic baskets and set out food on long tables the men and boys have carried into the school yard. There are hot dogs, rings of Lebanon bologna, red beet eggs, potato chips, pickles, potato salad, pretzels, cookies, pies, homemade root beer, and ice cream!

Once the tables are set, a father who is a minister gives the blessing. With the "amen" the children pile their plates high. Reuben wants only hot dogs and ice cream. Today, he gets his wish.

Anna goes through the line with the other sixth-grade girls. They find a grassy spot under the apple tree. Sitting, they tuck their bare feet under their dresses, balancing their plates in their laps. In the shade they eat, talk, and laugh.

Their plates empty, Anna and Mary return for dessert. At the table, Anna's young brother, David, is playing with his toy horses. A chocolate cookie crumb lies behind one horse. Anna nudges Mary. *"Haufa mischt,"* ("horse manure") she says, and they both giggle.

After eating, everyone goes inside for the program. The children recite poems, sing songs, and perform brief skits for their families.

Then it's outside for games. In one game the children must eat crackers and then try to whistle. Reuben sprays a shower of cracker bits as he tries.

For another game Fannie has taped balloons to two rows of chairs. Divided into two teams, the children try to break the balloons by sitting on them. *Pop-pop-pop!* the balloons burst. But the little ones have a time hoisting themselves on top of the balloons, and then some aren't heavy enough to burst the balloons just by sitting on them. They have to *rutch* around to get them to break.

Rooster Fight

This game is played by two teams with an equal number of players in lines facing one another. The teacher places numbers for the total number of children in each line in a hat and each child draws a number.

The two sides might look like this:

5–18–7–12–1–6–15–11–2–9–17–3–8–13–4–10–14–16

9–14–4–10–8–2–18–16–7–6–13–3–5–11–1–12–15–17

Between the two lines Fannie has placed a handkerchief under a paper plate. When she calls a number, say, five, the children on each side with the number five rush to the center to get the handkerchief. If one person can get the handkerchief and get back into line without being tagged by the other person, then that child's line gets a letter, *R*. But if the child who gets the handkerchief first is tagged, then the other side gets the letter. The game continues until one side is able to spell Rooster Fight.

Last is a baseball game with fathers and a few mothers against the boys and a few girls. In the field, Anna drops a pop-up and another ball rolls between her legs, but no one says anything. When her team finally gets the third out, they're behind only nine to nothing.

At bat, Anna makes up for her lack of fielding. She smacks the ball into right field for a triple and scores when Stevie slugs the ball over the fence into the nearby pasture. Anna scores three more times as the children win, twenty-nine to twenty-eight.

The games continue until it's time to milk the cows. After fathers and the boys load the benches and tables into the wagons, twelve teams head for home.

SUMMER

eⵔⵔ∘O∘O∘Oⵔ

Once the fields have been planted, a farmer's days become less hectic. There's still some tilling that must be done, but that's another job the children enjoy. Amos hitches a tiller to a driving horse, then Anna rides the horse bareback, carefully guiding it between the rows.

Summer evenings are often a time for fun. One evening Amos has a good idea. "Let's go fishing!" he says. Levi, Anna, and Amos find plenty of worms under the manure pile. Then Levi hitches Skip to the spring wagon. Once Anna and Amos climb in, he slaps the reins and Skip trots off down the dirt lane between the cornfields to John King's place.

As Levi ties Skip to a post near the Kings' barn, Anna and Amos jump out. Carrying their fishing poles and a can of worms, they open the gate to John King's pasture. The cows stop grazing and stare sleepily, as if they're trying to figure out who has come to visit.

The three crawl between the strands of the barbed-wire fence and climb the embankment at the edge of the woods. Over the crest of the ridge lies the pale green pond, disturbed only by an occasional bull's-eye ripple of a fish taking an insect.

Levi goes to the far end of the pond, where it is deeper. "I want to catch one of those big catfish," he says. Anna and Amos are content to fish for the bluegills and sunnies that cluster about the bulrushes and lily pads near the bank. Amos puts the worm on his hook and whips his rod over his shoulder and forward again. The line slaps into the water.

"Gut Himmel!" ("Good Heavens!") Levi exclaims. *"Net so hatt"* ("Not so hard").

Anna takes her time putting the slippery worm onto the hook. Gently she lowers her line into the water. Quickly, two fish rush over to inspect the interesting morsel. When Anna lifts her line from the water, only a bare hook remains.

Amos yanks his line from the water as if he had a whale on the other end. There's nothing but a clean hook dangling from the end of his line, too.

After splashing his line into the water a few more times, Amos catches a sunny. He yanks the little fish out of the water in a big arc, flopping it onto the grassy bank. Struggling with the hook, Amos finally frees the fish and drops it into a big bucket filled with water.

Soon Anna calls, *"Guck, der Fisch!"* ("Look, a fish!") as she carefully raises her rod. A little bluegill wiggles at the end of the line. She unhooks the fish and releases it in the bucket.

"Amos, *ich hop der gross Fisch!"* ("I have a big fish!") Levi shouts across the pond. Amos drops his line and races around the bank. Levi pulls hard. Amos thinks Levi has caught his hook on the bottom of the pond, but Levi's line moves back and forth. He continues to reel it in. About three yards away the water boils and Amos knows he has a big one.

An Amish boy tills a field of peppers while his sister, riding bareback, guides the horse through the rows. The little white tents shield the delicate plants from possible late frost.

Wrestling the fish onto the bank, Levi says, *"En Katzfisch!"* ("A cat-fish!"). Taking care not to get "stung" by the sharp dorsal fin, Levi unhooks the fish and lays it on the grass. The fish seems to smile at the boys as it twitches its whiskers. Handling the big fish gingerly, Levi slips it into the bucket, too.

Distant thunder tumbles down the valley like the roll of a kettle drum. Levi sees a yellow-white bolt of lightning slice from a large blue cloud, drilling into the earth. He counts, *"Eens, zwee, drei, vier, fimf, sex, siwwe, acht, nein, zehe, elf, zwelf, dreizeh, vazeh, fuffseh, sechzeh, siwwezeh, achtzeh, neinzeh, zwansich. Fimf Meile aveck.* [Five miles away] *Mach schnell!"*

Anna and Amos scramble after Levi down the bank of the pond. Hobbling along like a wooden-legged sailor, Levi struggles with the bucket of fish, sloshing water onto the dusty path as well as onto his pant leg.

Levi cracks the reins, barely waiting for Anna and Amos to hoist themselves onto the rear of the spring wagon, and Skip breaks into a quick trot. Down the lane between the cornfields they speed. The wagon wheels crackle as they spin over the gravel path, sending out small plumes of dust. Levi urges Skip on as thunder and lightning seem to rumble toward them.

Levi cannot remember ever being so glad to reach the barnyard. As he unhitches Skip, Amos lifts the bucket from the wagon and pours the fish into the trough for the horses. There they'll eat the flies and spiders that fall in and clean the algae that builds up in the trough during the summer.

Just as Levi closes the barn door, a small funnel cloud spins through the gravel driveway, kicking up dust. Fat raindrops pelt his back as he dashes for the house. Safely inside, the children gather around the table, helping themselves to a snack of bologna, corn curls, and fruit drink Mamm has set out.

"Eenichebbes grickt?" ("Get anything?") Daat asks from behind his newspaper.

"Ya," Amos says, and tells Daat he'll show him the fish when the rain stops.

Suddenly the room lights up and booming thunder shakes the house, rattling the dishes in the cupboard and the china in the cabinet. Daat crinkles his newspaper, David spills his drink, Anna jumps off the bench, and Mamm gasps, crossing her arms over her chest. Daat rushes to the window to see if lightning has hit the barn.

Amish do not have lightning rods on their barns or homes. They believe that if lightning strikes a house or barn, it is the will of God. If the lightning causes a house or barn to burn to the ground, the people of the church help rebuild it. But a barn raising, at which a barn is built in one day, happens only after weeks of preparation: rebuilding the foundation and cutting the beams and trusses to the proper lengths.

Although they do not carry insurance, unfortunate Amishmen can receive assistance from "Amish Aid," a fund to which each family contributes for just such emergencies. In addition, relatives and friends will give some of their own possessions to an unlucky family.

"Ei yi, yi! Es hatt really gereggert," ("My, oh my! It really rains hard") says Daat, staring through the blurry window. He sees the cows huddled near the barn door, their rumps pointed into the teeth of the storm.

Now Daat worries: Will wind blow down his corn so it cannot pollinate, or will hail poke little holes in his peppers, ruining them? A farmer constantly worries about his crops. Late frosts, early frosts, too much rain, not enough rain, destructive storms, and hungry insects can mean the difference between bumper crops and disastrous losses.

The next day Daat's brother Abner drives down the lane. He tells

Daat that the wind blew down some of his corn. Those stalks are lost.
"But," Abner says, "Amos Stoltzfus"—who lives only two miles down
the road—"didn't get a drop!" They both shake their heads, puzzled
by weather's strange behavior.

Then Abner asks him if he would like to go look for a driving horse.
Daat thinks for a moment before agreeing to go. With the storm the
night before, it's too wet to make hay.

Daat invites Amos, Levi, and Anna to go along. Together, they set
off across the mountain to visit Aaron, their Mennonite friend who
deals in driving horses, much like a car dealer sells automobiles. Amish
need strong horses to pull their buggies. Just as you would prefer
riding in a nice car rather than in an old beat-up jalopy, no Amish, as
humble as they are, wants to drive a broken-down horse. That would
be a sign of a poor farmer. Amish like alert, spirited horses that hold
their heads high and lift their feet as they trot. And to pull a buggy
with a family, they must be gentle and not easily "spooked" or fright-
ened by passing cars. That's why most Amishmen prefer American
saddlebreds or standardbreds.

Daat and his brother walk through the stable, inspecting the horses.
They are not interested in those that look dull or have sad expressions.
They do not want horses with swaybacks or large heads. A light
chestnut horse neighs and comes over to greet Daat. He tells Aaron
he'd liked to try that one.

As Aaron hitches the horse to a two-wheeled wagon, Daat inspects
the young gelding, a male horse that has been neutered. Geldings are
easier than stallions to handle and are less high-strung. Daat looks in
the horse's mouth and he examines its legs, looking for any sign of
lameness. Sometimes unscrupulous horse dealers give a lame horse
drugs. When the drug wears off, the lameness returns and the new

owner is stuck. Aaron's an honest trader. But he has been tricked a few times himself. Now he buys only horses with papers, which show the pedigree and previous owners. Because the owners can be traced, a horse with papers is less likely to be lame.

Daat climbs in, slaps the reins, and takes off down the country road on a "test drive." He drives a few other horses, but in the end settles on the light chestnut gelding. After a little fussing, Daat and Aaron agree on a fair price.

The following day, when the horse is delivered, Daat hitches it to the spring wagon and gives everyone a ride. He tells Levi that it's his turn to name the new horse. Levi names him Star, for the white mark on his forehead.

One especially humid morning Anna sees the gray station wagon coming down the lane, churning great billows of dust. She rushes over to see her friend Elizabeth.

"Would you and your family like to go to the zoo today?" Elizabeth asks.

Elizabeth and Anna run inside to ask Daat.

"I think our work could wait another day. How soon do you want to leave?" he asks.

"About one o'clock," Elizabeth says.

"Fast time?" Anna asks, referring to daylight saving time. Amish do not observe daylight saving time but stay on eastern standard time all year-round.

"Yes, fast time. Twelve o'clock your time."

"That would be fine," Daat says.

After lunch, Anna, her brothers and sisters, Daat, and Mamm change from their work clothing into their "for good" clothing.

Squeezing into the station wagon, the two families drive over the mountain to the next valley where an "English" farmer has constructed a small petting zoo.

The children have fun feeding the animals—a contrary llama, some silly monkeys, and a goat who eats almost anything. It is too hot for the tree bears, who sleep. The African lion with a full shaggy mane stirs only when the zookeeper throws him a frozen chicken.

Daat does not like the snake, even though it is only a harmless garter snake.

Best of all for Anna and Elizabeth on this sultry day is the stop for tall cones of soft ice cream.

Two days later a searing summer sun creates heat waves over the fields. Hot, dry weather is good for making hay. Amos hitches Bob and Rock to the mower and cuts several fields of grass.

Once the grass has dried for a few days, Amos hitches up Charlie and Jerry to a side delivery rake that piles the hay into rows so it can be scooped up by the baler.

The next day Daat hitches up Jim and Betsy to pull a baler powered by a small gasoline engine. Then he hooks a wagon behind it. Daat will drive the baler while Amos stacks the bales on the wagon. Anna and Rebecca hitch Bob and Rock to another hay wagon. She and Rebecca help her little brother, carrying a jug of ice water, and her little sister, with a bundle of books, onto the empty wagon. Then she guides the big Belgians into the shade of the big oaks at the end of the lane.

At the far end of the field, the baler scoops hay into its jaws. Soon a bale pushes out the back. Amos muscles the bales onto the wagon, stacking them.

As they wait for Amos to pile the wagon full of bales, Anna and Rebecca read stories to their little brother and sister. Just as Anna finishes *A Kiss for Little Bear,* she notices that Daat and Amos have stopped baling. The hay wagon is full.

Anna helps her little brother and sister hop off their hay wagon. They are told to sit under the oak tree and look at the rest of the books.

Anna and Rebecca take their wagon to the baler. Amos now unhitches Bob and Rock from the empty wagon and hitches them to the full wagon and drives them to the barn, where he will unload the bales.

Daat hooks the empty wagon behind the baler. Together, Anna and Rebecca will stack bales until Amos comes back to help.

The hazy yellow sun climbs high in the summer sky. Stacking bales of hay is hard work. Soon everyone, except David and Sarah under the shade tree, is sweating. But Amish do not take off their shirts and they never wear shorts. They only roll up their sleeves. For one thing, stripping down like that would be showing off one's body and Amish do not believe in that. But shirts with sleeves and long pants are best for working in the hay fields, because dry hay is scratchy and workers get covered with a fine, itchy dust.

Everyone, though, is barefooted, even Daat.

Amos returns with the wagon empty, having unloaded the bales in the barn. Daat says it's time for a break. Under the oaks they rest and drink ice-cold spring water. Anna pours a little water onto a small cut on her foot that must have come from a stiff weed or sharp stone.

Soon it is back to work.

That evening Elizabeth comes to see if Anna can play. If she were at home, Elizabeth might suggest they ride bicycles. Amish children do not have bicycles, but they do ride wagons and scooters. No one seems to know why wagons and scooters are all right while bicycles are not. That's just the way things are.

Sarah and David are playing Horsey. Sarah has tied a rope around

Often the whole Amish family works together. In the summertime they make enough hay to last their animals throughout the winter.

David. She gives the "reins" a jiggle and David trots around the yard. "Whoa!" she calls, pulling hard on the reins. David stops. Sarah lifts his foot and pretends to clean a stone from David's "hoof."

Anna and Elizabeth decide to play Indian Tag with Amos and Rebecca. Anna is "it," but it doesn't take her long to tag Rebecca on the arm. Rebecca must now hold her arm at the place where her sister tagged her and try to tag someone else. Soon everybody is holding an arm or leg. But when Amos tags Rebecca, who is now holding both arms on her leg, she can no longer run and is out of the game.

Later Anna and Rebecca play London Bridge with the garden hose. At the water trough Amos fills a water pistol and gets an unsuspecting Levi in the back of the neck. Soon a water battle breaks out. By the time Mamm calls, they are soaked.

AUTUMN

By Labor Day it's time to pick the peppers. Everyone helps, even Mamm and little David and Sarah. Every once in a while they stand and arch their backs. Stooping over to pick peppers is very hard work. By the end of the day, they think they may never stand straight again.

In the evening Anna reads from *Night Markets.* " 'You don't come to Hunts Point to buy a few apples or tomatoes. Peek inside the warehouse and you'll find a mountain of onions or a sea of watermelons.' "

"Hunts Point," Anna exclaims. "That's where we send our peppers!"

The Amish do not observe Halloween. They do not believe in ghosts, goblins, or ghouls. Such creatures were conjured up by early pagans and therefore are not Christian symbols. But late on the evening of October 31, Anna finds some old clothing, fashions herself a costume, and runs around the house scaring her little brother and sisters.

Amish do celebrate Thanksgiving, but without all the festivities. Rather, it is a quiet day for visiting friends and relatives.

WINTER

◦○◦○◦○◦

Once winter arrives, life on the farm slows. On a Saturday afternoon, Amish children head for the frozen ponds. While the girls skate around together, the boys get up a hockey game.

Twilight angles across the fields, casting long shadows. Approaching the winter solstice—December 21, the shortest day of the year—the sun sets early, before the evening chores are done.

Christmas for the Amish is a two-day affair, Christmas and the day after. But for the children, the celebration begins with a program on the afternoon of Christmas Eve. A week earlier, the children exchanged pieces of paper with their names on them. This morning they enter school excited, carrying their small gifts.

Anna and Sadie help Fannie hand out the gifts. Anna, who is always writing letters during her free time, receives writing paper from Sadie. Anna flashes a smile of appreciation to Sadie. Then Anna watches Susie Beiler as she opens her present, a needlepoint kit that Anna got her. Anna answers Susie's thank-you with another smile.

Amish girls skate around the boys playing hockey. The pair of sneakers on the ice marks the goal.

After lunch, parents crowd into the one-room schoolhouse as the children perform small plays. Some are about Christ's birth, but some are just for fun.

In one skit, Rachel makes soup for Lydia, who is coming to visit. Malinda tells Rachel it needs salt, but Rachel is busy. Katie tastes the soup, says it needs salt, but Rachel is busy. Sarah tastes the soup, says it needs salt, but Rachel is busy.

Later, Malinda returns, tastes the soup, notices it still needs salt, and adds some. Katie knows that Rachel didn't have time to add salt, so she adds a pinch of salt. Sarah also knows Rachel was busy and adds some salt. Rachel finishes her cleaning and, as she passes the stove, remembers to add some salt.

The children and parents howl when Lydia, played by Anna, sits down and takes a sip of this very salty soup.

Following the skits, parents and children join in singing Christmas carols, and the children present their parents with small gifts they made in school. Then it's time for Christmas cookies and punch.

Today, instead of boarding the school bus, the children climb in their buggies, laughing and talking all the way home.

Christmas morning begins not with opening presents around a Christmas tree but with a regular church service. The minister reads the accounts of Christ's birth from the book of Luke and delivers a sermon on the Christmas story. Then it's time for visiting and a wonderful Christmas dinner.

Amish do not believe in Santa Claus and they do not put up a Christmas tree. But just as the Wise Men gave the Christ Child gifts of gold, frankincense, and myrrh, Amish parents give their children modest presents. Anna receives a horse calendar; Levi, a hockey stick; Amos, a pocket knife; Rebecca, a sled; Sarah, a baby doll; and David, more horses for his toy barn.

Christmas evening Elizabeth and her family visit. Elizabeth gives Anna a special present, a stuffed toy beaver she made in her home-economics sewing class. Anna gives Elizabeth a little calendar with a border of braided yarn.

Throughout the evening no one passing the kitchen table spread with plate upon plate of Christmas cookies can resist snitching just one more. Anna and Elizabeth help themselves to some chocolate-chip cookies and a few sand tarts. Soon both families gather around the warmth of the wood stove to listen to Elizabeth read *Babushka,* a

Russian folktale with a Christmas message. Then Anna's mother leads everyone in singing Christmas carols: "Silent Night," "Away in the Manger," "The Friendly Beasts," "Once in David's Royal City," and many others.

At the end of the evening, Anna walks Elizabeth out to her family's car. The deep black winter night sparkles with stars.

"Merry Christmas," Anna says with a smile.

"Un hallich Nei Yaahr," Elizabeth says, waving good-bye.

Next page: The winter sun sets early, just as an Amish boy completes his evening chores.

BIBLIOGRAPHY

◦C◦C◦C◦C◦

Brand, Millen. *Fields of Peace.* Garden City, N.Y.: Doubleday, 1970.

Fisher, Sara E., and Rachel K. Stahl. *The Amish School.* Intercourse, Pa.: Good Books, 1986.

Fretz, Clarence Y., ed. *Anabaptist Hymnal.* Hagerstown, Md.: Deutsche Buchhandlung, 1987.

Hostetler, John A. *Amish Life.* Scottdale, Pa.: Herald Press, 1983.

———. *Amish Society.* Baltimore: The Johns Hopkins University Press, 1981.

Hostetler, John A., and Gertrude Enders Huntington. *Children in Amish Society.* New York: Holt, Rinehart & Winston, 1971.

Klees, Fredric. *The Pennsylvania Dutch.* New York: Macmillan, 1950.

Lee, Douglas. "The Plain People of Pennsylvania." *National Geographic,* April 1984, 492–519.

Rice, Charles S., and Rollin Steinmetz. *The Amish Year.* New Brunswick, N.J.: Rutgers University Press, 1956.

Scott, Stephen. *Plain Buggies.* Intercourse, Pa.: Good Books, 1981.

———. *Why Do They Dress That Way?* Intercourse, Pa.: Good Books, 1986.

CHILDREN'S BOOKS ABOUT THE AMISH

De Angeli, Marguerite. *Henner's Lydia.* Garden City, N.Y.: Doubleday, 1937.

————. *Yonie Wondernose.* Garden City, N.Y.: Doubleday, 1944.

Foster, Sally. *Where Time Stands Still.* New York: Dodd, Mead, 1987.

Israel, Fred. *Meet the Amish.* New York: Chelsea House, 1986.

Lenski, Lois. *Shoo-Fly Girl.* Philadelphia: Lippincott, 1963.

Meyer, Carolyn. *Amish People: Plain Living in a Complex World.* New York: Atheneum, 1976.

Naylor, Phyllis Reynolds. *An Amish Family.* New York: Lamplight Publishing, 1974.

Steffy, Jan. *The School Picnic.* Intercourse, Pa.: Good Books, 1987.

Yoder, Carolyn P. *Cobblestone: The History Magazine for Young People.* November 1987.

Yoder, Joseph W. *Rosanna of the Amish.* Scottdale, Pa.: Herald Press, 1973.

BOOKS CITED IN TEXT

Farley, Walter. *Black Stallion.* New York: Random House, 1941.

Henry, Marguerite. *King of the Wind.* New York: Rand McNally, 1948.

Horwitz, Joshua. *Night Markets.* New York: Crowell, 1984.

Mikolaycak, Charles. *Babushka.* New York: Holiday House, 1984.

Minarik, Else Homelund. *A Kiss for Little Bear.* New York: Harper & Row, 1968.

Paulsen, Gary. *Hatchet.* New York: Bradbury, 1985.

Purdy, Carol. *Least of All.* New York: Margaret K. McElderry, 1987.

Sewell, Anna. *Black Beauty.* New York: World Publishing, 1972.

Wilder, Laura Ingalls. *Little House on the Prairie.* New York: Harper & Row, 1935.

COOKBOOKS

Big Valley Amish Cook Book. Gordonville, Pa.: Print Shop, 1979.

Groff, Betty, and Jose Wilson. *Good Earth Country and Cooking.* Harrisburg, Pa.: Stackpole Books, 1974.

Showalter, Mary Emma. *Mennonite Community Cookbook.* Scottdale, Pa.: The Mennonite Community Associates, 1969.

INDEX

99